WITHDRAWN
FROM THE
MERTON PUBLIC
LIBRARIES.

KU-470-597

THIS. BOOK BELONGS
TO

Other Fun & Puzzle books available in Armada

2nd Armada Book of Jokes and Riddles
Crazy – But True!
compiled by Jonathan Clements

The Awful Joke Book
The Most Awful Joke Book Ever
The Batty Book Book
The Batty Cartoon Book
How Trivial Can You Get?
edited by Mary Danby

The Explorer's Handbook
The Secret Agent's Handbook
The Spookster's Handbook
The Trickster's Handbook
The Whizzkid's Handbooks 1–3
The Whizzkid's Whizzbook
compiled by Peter Eldin

The Great Spy Race
Puzzlequest 1
Michael Holt

The Grisly Joke Book
compiled by David Pugh

THE RIDDLE OF
THE SPHINX

Michael Holt

Illustrated by
Marilyn Day

WITHDRAWN FROM THE MERTON PUBLIC LIBRARIES

Wimbledon Park Library,
Arthur Road,
London, SW19 8AD.
Tel. No. 946

A J Q 1117

An Armada Original

The Riddle of the Sphinx was first published
in Armada in 1987 by Fontana Paperbacks,
8 Grafton Street, London W1X 3LA

Armada is an imprint of
Fontana Paperbacks, part of
the Collins Publishing Group.

© Michael Holt 1987
© Illustrations Marilyn Day 1987

Printed in Great Britain by
William Collins Sons & Co. Ltd. Glasgow

Conditions of Sale
This book is sold subject to the condition
that it shall not, by way of trade or otherwise,
be lent, re-sold, hired out or otherwise circulated
without the publisher's prior consent in any form of
binding or cover other than that in which it is
published and without a similar condition
including this condition being imposed
on the subsequent purchaser.

THE RIDDLE OF THE SPHINX

Welcome to the world of Puzzlequest, a world of espionage and intrigue, where treachery knows no bounds. You, Alex, have been summoned to M Fifteen, the world-famous spy headquarters where the Head of Secret Operations, N, is ready with your orders.

N has a very special assignment for you this time involving the Master Spy Count Jugula and his bungling accomplices Amadeus, Wolf-fang and Mozart – code-named the Mozart trio. The Count is after the famous Egyptian Scarab – an engraved beetle-shaped gem which holds the secret of World Power. He'll stop at nothing to possess it – and if he succeeds, well, shall we say, life will never be quite the same again.

You will travel to Cairo, the heart of pyramid land, across the desert – but the many hazards you encounter will leave little time for sight-seeing. At critical stages of your journey you will be forced to unravel ingenious puzzles. Each correct answer will immediately send you on the next stage of your quest. However, each time you fail to answer correctly, you will be sent on a detour and faced with even more brain-teasers to solve. You will also have lost valuable time so remember to THINK before attempting each puzzle.

You won't be alone on your travels as you'll have the expert help of your trusty mongrel, Mugs. You will also encounter a host of other characters on the way including the well known magicman Saul Spaniels (whom you'll like . . . but not a lot!) the voracious Virginia Werewolf and the Count's retired vampire turned servant, Bludsucker. Each one will be trying to test you and it is for you to decide whether to believe the information they feed you.

Oh, I nearly forgot, in the unlikely event of you not wanting to play exactly by the rules, there is a special section at the back of the book for that lowly breed of humans – *CHEATS*. It lists all the answers to every puzzle just in case you get stuck. But a word of advice for those of you with espionage ambitions: rule number one in *The Spy's Handbook* is trust no one (not even yourself!) and never leave yourself open to compromise.

Hurry, Alex, there are spies to be caught!

The phone rings. You are relaxing after tea in your flat which you share with your faithful hound, Mugs.

"Alex?" the phone barks. Mugs barks back.

"Ssssh!" you say.

"Don't you shush me!" the phone crackles.

"Er, not *you*, sir!" you stammer into the phone. It is N, your boss at M 15. M Fifteen is the code name for MI 5, the Spy-Catching Circus. You haven't talked to N for at least twenty four hours. That was when N sent you on holiday after your last successful adventure.

"Ah," the phone rasps in your ear, "not gone on holiday yet, I see."

"How did you guess, sir?"

The voice replies suavely, "When you've been in the spy business as long as me, you get to suss these things . . ."

"Gosh!" you say, in admiration of N's shrewdness.

"Get over here AT ONCE!" The phone goes dead.

You check the time on your radio clock. 6 p.m. What *can* N want you for at this hour. It must be pretty serious.

You and Mugs reach the Spy Circus in record time. You let yourself in by a shabby side door of a gaunt Victorian building. You climb to the sixth floor by a rickety lift. You leave the lift and walk the length of a dark corridor. Without knocking, you swing into N's vast office. Far away across an expanse of thick pile carpet you spot N. He is peering intently into a goldfish bowl. You cough to announce your presence.

"Ah, you got here," N says absently. "A little problem for you, Alex. It is Alex, isn't it?"

"Something pretty serious, is it, sir?" you say.

"Actually, yes, old thing," N admits. "If I put my finger in this goldfish bowl, which has a goldfish swimming in it, will it weigh more?"

"Your finger, sir?" you enquire politely. "Or the goldfish?"

"Neither, you blithering idiot." N spits out. "The goldfish bowl of water!"

If you don't think the goldfish bowl of water weighs more, go to **85**.

If you do, go to **98**.

If you think N is living in a goldfish bowl, go to **71**.

2

Smart guess. But not smart enough. 3 won't give a whole number of cats. Go back to **46**.

3

"Yes, 11 o'clock," Bludsucker agrees. "Time for a puzzle. And then I'm off to bed," he says, putting nine matches on the bar. "Can you make three squares with these nine matches?"

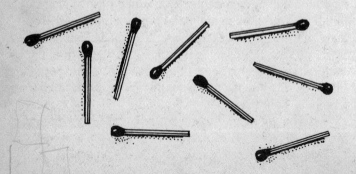

For the answer, guess which to go to: **82**
28
90

4

You say, "Did you say 'Umbo'?" Whatever the native now replies will be the word meaning "Yes".
Now you can try again at **115**. This time try working out the *differences* between next-door numbers on the dial.

5

35 is right! Now go back to **39** and have another try.

6

No. There were 35 triangles. Now go back to **39**.

It should be your original number. Wanna know how it works?

Think it's mind-reading? Go to **148**.
Or is it number trickery? Go to **55**.

Wrong room. Go back to **111**.

The decoded message reads:
    SEE WAX PANE IN SPHINX'S PAW

"The Sphinx!" you exclaim. "We must go to the Sphinx at once. Cairo, here we come! C'mon, Mugs. We must fly – to Cairo – before Mozart and Co get there."

In flight to Cairo you jot N a cheery card and draw two patterns on it. One of them contains the shape known as a *Sphinx*.

"That should tell N where we are going," you whisper to Mugs. "But it must be in code."

"Of *course*," Mugs sniffs.

Which pattern has a sphinx in it?
Is it A? Go to **146**.
Is it B? Go to **136**.

A

Dear N,
Having a
great time.
Alex and
Mugs

POST
CARD

B

"Ten rungs," you say easily to Mara. "In fact, ma'am, the same number as are high 'n' dry now, for the paddle-boat rises with the water."

You wander along to the bar. Before you can order a drink, the bar fills up with people who want to fill themselves up. You spot Amadeus, Wolf-fang, Bludsucker in a white pith helmet, and . . .

Mozart. The *real* Mozart!

Here is a snapshot of the group and another showing a number of differences. How many can you detect? Go to the section with the same number of differences.

Need help? Go to **29**.

"Eleven ways!" you decide. "Bludsucker can have taken any one of them. Too many to catch him."

At Cairo Railway Station you book straight through to Memphis. You descend from the train at Memphis. Your gaze is met not by the wonders of Ancient Egypt but by a modern wonder – the beautiful international lady spy, Mara Harti. She stands well over 6 feet, slinky, dark-eyed and long-haired. You slip on the latex mask of Mozart that N chucked at you. You advance on her confidently.

She extends a hand with long red nails. "I'm Mara Harti," she growls in a gravelly voice. "Mr Mozart, I presume."

You bow with old-world courtesy. Mugs doggedly bow-wows.

Mara croons sinisterly, "Your two friends, Amadeus and Wolf-fang, are aboard the paddle boat now. Count Jugula will be joining us at Luxor."

"Why, are we coming apart?" you smile. She bares her teeth. This wipes the smile off your latex face.

A short camel ride brings you to the River Nile. And to the moored paddle-boat with its gaily striped awnings. As you stride up the gang-plank, Mara leading the way, you spot a rope ladder dangling from the boat in the water. Ten of its equally-spaced rungs are clear of the water. Each is 10 centimetres apart, you note like a true detective.

"All aboard!" the Captain calls. "The Nile is in flood. The water's rising fast."

"How fast?" you enquire.

"About 10 centimetres an hour," the Captain replies. "High water will be at midnight tonight." You check your watch – it is four o'clock.

"Tell me, Mr Mozart," Mara coos like a vulture, "how many rungs will be clear of the water at midnight tonight?" She bows. You shudder, and the bows of the paddle-boat begin to shudder too.

Go to the section with the same number as there are rungs showing above the water.

Swamped? Need help? Have you *rung* up N? Do, on **73**.

12

You nip back to the airport. You find the Left Luggage Lockers. And there it is, Locker Number 12.

You open it with the standard skeleton spy key N supplied you with. Inside you find nothing but a tatty bit of paper. On it is what looks like a sum – except it is written in letters:

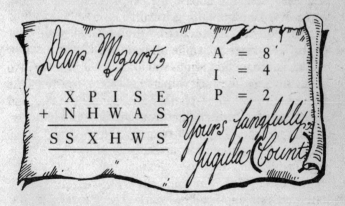

Obviously, each letter stands for one number.

If you think HWS stands for 639,   go to **103**
If you think it stands for 391,   go to **170**
Or if you think it stands for 561,   go to **60**.

13

Longer, longer! Go back to **70**.

14

No, try again. Back to **102**.

15

Yes, there are fifteen differences. You glance round at the motley if not bottled – er mottled – crew. Bludsucker is thoroughly enjoying acting up in his light disguise of an English colonel, complete with white ducks and sola topee and false moustache.

Mara calls across to Bludsucker, "Hullo! I like your white ducks."

"Yes," Wolf-fang quips, "they make you look like Francis *Drake*!"

While everyone is chatting, you are feverishly deciding what to do: to take the mask off and reveal your true identity or to bluff it out. The decision is taken out of your hands. You happen to be standing in front of a looking glass. Mozart – the *real* Mozart – wanders over to comb his hair.

You stand in front of the mirror and pretend to be his reflection.

Here is a picture of Mozart and also of three different poses you could take up, wearing his latex mask, of course.

Which reflection will Mozart expect to see in the mirror?

If you think the right reflection is face A,   go to **104**

If you think it is face B,   go to **81**

Or if you think it is face C,   go to **40**.

A

B

C

16

It should be your original number. Wanna know how it works?

Think it's mind-reading?   Go to **148**.

Or is it number trickery?   Go to **55**.

17

No, they weren't. Go back to **121** and try again.

18

Actually there is a simple way. Try revolving the inner triangle through a third of a full turn. Can you see it now? Go back to **76**.

19

The nineteen moves are: Step 1, step back to floor, 1 again, 2, 3, down to 2, 3, 4, 5, down to 4, 5, 6, 7, down to 6, 7, 8, landing, down to 8, landing. There!

"Thank you," Bludsucker says. "I've always wanted to know . . . ever since my master, Count Jugula, first sent me here to find the Secret of World Power. Jolly stuffy place. Let's get out."

You emerge into the bright, bright sunlight. Bludsucker closes the panel behind you. You are standing by the Sphinx's south paw. With one hand on his gun keeping you covered, he grasps the gold box in the other. He asks you to hold his gun a moment while he opens the box. You take the gun and shout: "Stick 'em up!"

Bludsucker laughs in your face. "It's not loaded."

He feverishly opens the box with the key you selected. Inside is a small compartment. In that is a green Scarab beetle and a visiting card, printed Count Jugula on one side. On the other is a message. Bludsucker takes one look at it, drops the card, and runs off with the gold box of the Scarab. He leaps into a waiting taxi shouting, "Cairo, the railway station!" and disappears in a dust-storm of sand.

You stoop to pick up the card. You read what terrified him so:

$$
\begin{array}{r}
FLY \\
FOR \\
+ YOUR \\
\hline LIFE
\end{array}
\qquad
\begin{array}{l}
F = 5 \\
Y = 8 \\
E = 2
\end{array}
$$

Below the sum is a message, in code:

598 TO 94X07

"First we must complete the sum, Mugs," you say. "Then we can crack the code."

Where does the message tell you to go to?

LOXUR?   Go to **66**.
LUXOR?   Go to **78**.
RUXOL?   Go to **32**.

20

No. There were 35 triangles. Now go back to **39**.

21

You've lost your way. Go back to **149** and try again.

22

No, too few. That way you might not get a matching pair of left and right hand gloves. Go to **37**.

23

You race to the Amusement Arcade down the hot, busy road thronging with Egyptians. You make for Space Invaders Machine Number 23. Mozart's dead letter drop! Tucked behind the machine is a note with important information which you will learn by solving this puzzle:

Find the missing word in each everyday phrase. Write it in its numbered row of boxes *below*. The arrowed column will spell where you go next.

1 break the ——'s back (overload)
2 without a moment's —— (instantly)
3 in the —— of time (narrowly)
4 chew the —— (chat)
5 rub the —— way (upset)
6 a storm in a —— cup (a lot of fuss over a trifle)
7 hold one's —— (keep silent)

Where do you go next? The theatre?   Go to **112**
Or maybe the pyramid?   Go to **74**
Or do you go to the minaret?   Go to **58**.

24

No, it is a moth. Try again at **58**.

Scratched on a pillar in the temple you see a magic symbol. "The witch's pentacle," you cry. "We must see how many triangles are in the design or else . . ." How many triangles can you see?

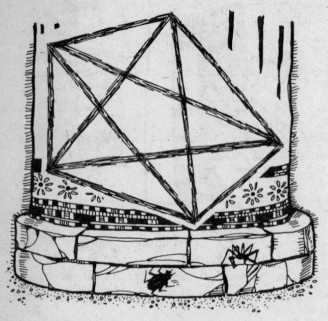

If you think there are 35?   Go to **5**
If you think there are 30?   Go to **6**
Or if you think there are 25? Go to **20**.

26

No, fewer moves. Step lively! This is the rule: You return to the floor after the first step; then go three steps up for one step down. Go back to **140**.

No, he didn't. Go back to **63**.

Fooled you! No, go to **54**.

Between 13 and 16 differences. Go back to **10**.

Tricky one, this. Don't lose any sleep over it – just go back to **56** and try again.

"20 hours," you reply correctly.

"Dare say you're right," Bludsucker replies as an Arab boy enters the bar with a trayful of green Scarab beetles. Bludsucker starts. Can they be replicas of the Scarab beetle he has only just purloined from the gold box from the Sphinx's paw? Surely not.

"Genuine Arab Scarab," the Arab whines, "from Pharaoh's tomb. Only 20 piastres each."

Bludsucker buys one instantly. Then he thinks better of it and sells it for 30 piastres to Amadeus who ambles into the bar at that instant. A little later Amadeus sells it for 40 piastres back to Bludsucker, who tends to be forgetful. Soon after Wolf-fang strolls in and Bludsucker sells it to him for 50 piastres.

How much profit did Bludsucker make?

20 piastres?   Go to **65**
0 piastres?   Go to **72**
10 piastres?   Go to **116**

32

Got your sums wrong, Alex. Go back to **19**. Clue: 598
means FLY. Now the sum should be plain sailing.

33

No. Before you try again, see if you can do any better with
this one.

All these names were given to one machine at one time
or another. Count up the numbers of the correct answers:
bone-shaker   dandy-horse   hobby-horse   penny-
farthing
What was the machine?
an automobile (2)   a bicycle (5)   a motorbike (20)

What does LCD mean?
Local Council Dustbins (26) Low Cholesterol Decibels
(11) Liquid Crystal Display (18)

Which of these is *not* a child's toy?
Dingbot (8)   Omnibot (29)   Zoid (14)   Smackbot (24)
  If you score 47, go to **67**.
  If you score 49, go to **155**.

34

No, they weren't. Go back to **121** and try again.

Intrepid explorers that you are, you and Mugs push on into the jungle. N has primed you in a little Umbobo, the local jungle lingo. Trouble is you can't remember which word means "Yes" and which means "No". One is "Umbo", the other's "Bobo".

As luck has it, you meet a rested native in a clearing. In perfect Umbobo you ask, "Is this the way to the waterfall?"

"Umbo!" the native says gleefully.

What four words can you ask next to find out if he said "Yes" or "No" in Umbobo?

Guess: go to **4** or to **169**.

No, too few. You might not get a matching pair that way of left and right hand gloves. Go to **37**.

You ask a lady tourist if she has seen three suspicious-looking men. (The Mozart Trio, in other words.) But she is deep in a puzzle in her newspaper. So you help her solve it. This is it:

Start at any letter. Spell up, down, sideways, or on the slant. How many girl's names can you spell?

10–14?   Go to **167**
15–19?   Go to **127**

You and Mugs wake up next morning to find the paddle steamer drawing in to Luxor. As the steamer pulls into the bank, you two are the first ashore.

"We must keep a keen eye out for Count Jugula," you tell Mugs.

Soon you are wandering among the broken blocks lying in the sand of once-proud temples. You find an old soothsayer sitting by a curious circle of symbols scratched on an old column lying in the sand:

"Choose any two-figure number," the soothsayer says. "The figures must be different, for example 33 won't do. Now reverse the figures. Take the smaller figure from the bigger. (If you had chosen 27, you'd get 72 and then take 27 from 72 which gives you 45.) Now add the two figures you get in your result. (You'd add 4 to the 5.) And hold that answer in your head."

The soothsayer points to the strange circle of symbols. "Tap the vampire symbol at the top and call it 'One'. Now count round clockwise and go on till you reach the number in your head. Stop there."

You do so, Alex.

The soothsayer says: "And I predict you will stop at . . .

Which symbol will it be? The axe?	Go to **174**
Will it be the dagger?	Go to **45**
Or will it be the bat?	Go to **33**

39

You fly to Lake Victoria. You listen in on your short-wave radio. You overhear Count Jugula talking to Bludsucker aboard their ship, the *S. S. Titania*, in the middle of the lake.

"Those dratted spy-catchers!" the Count curses. (He means you and Mugs.) "We must hide the lake."

"Hide the lake?" Bludsucker asks. "But it is 100 miles across."

"Easy," the Count replies. "We'll plant a fast-growing Victoria Lily in the middle. It doubles its size every hour. It'll cover the lake in twenty five hours."

"Won't we need time to manoeuvre the ship?" Bludsucker asks.

"Right!" the Count shouts. "After how many hours

will it cover half the lake?"

"Let me see," Bludsucker mumbles, "should be as easy as pie. That's it! Pi R squared . . . or something . . ."

How long will the lily take to cover half the lake? You can assume the lake is circular and that Pi is 22/7.

Is it $\dfrac{25 \times Pi \times 50^2}{2}$? Go to **122**

Or is it 24 hours? Go to **173**.

40

No, Mozart would see through that! The eyebrows are the wrong way round. Go back to **15**.

41

Shorter, shorter! Go back to **70**.

42

Take a hint: There are more than ten ways from Cairo to Memphis. Go back to **78** and try again. One more time! (That's a clue.)

43

Correct. The answers were: Countess, Thirty-nine and gander. Now go back to **56** and have another try.

44

No, it should be your original number. See if you can do any better with this one.

What is a light year? (A) a period of time? or (B) a

measure of distance or (C) a degree of illumination?

A go to **137**
B go to **132**.
C go to **59**.

45

Mugs cocked his head to one side as if to say: "Wonder how the soothsayer knew you'd pick the dagger . . .' You have no time to answer for suddenly you see an army lorry speed off into the distance . . . Driving it is the Count. He has the precious Scarab. Mugs pricks up his ears and runs after the departing lorry. Soon he comes trotting back, bearing a sheet of paper.

You snatch it from him excitedly.

"It's a message for Bludsucker," you exclaim, "telling him where to meet the Count."

This is what you read:

Put the answer to each clue in the numbered rows of boxes. When filled in properly, the arrowed column will tell you where to go.

1. Turn CANOE into a vast body of water.
2. Change DEAL into a dense metal.
3. Turn STREAM into a teacher.
4. Turn DUAL into praise.
5. Change TUTOR into a fish.
6. Change RATE into rent.
7. Turn SCOPE into a thicket.
8. Turn STEP into a nuisance.

Where do you go to meet the count?
To the catacomb? **175**
To the catapult? **177**
To the cataract? **121**.
"Won't catch me out!" Mugs wags his tail smugly.

46

"Yes," Bludsucker says, "a pith helmet. Pithy, eh what?"

Amadeus nudges Wolf-fang. "He's off! Let's sit back and enjoy the show. You know what a show-off he is."

Bludsucker goes on: "For my next puzzle, ladeez and ge'men, I'd like you to watch my sola topee closely. No sir, not my one and only, my sole toupé. I don't wear a wig! In this hat I have several cats—"

"How many?" Mugs barks excitedly.

Bludsucker stares into the hat and pretends to count cats. "Umm . . . ah yes! two-thirds of their number plus two thirds of a cat. And I assure you all, no cruelty is involved. I can state CATegorically that the answer's a whole number of cats."

How many cats has Bludsucker got in his hat?

If you think it's 2 cats,   go to **147**
If you think it's 3 cats,   go to **2**
Or if you think it's 4 cats,   go to **93**.

47

Wrong room. Go back to **111**.

48

No. It was a black cat. Now go back to **9** and have another look at that code.

49

Wrong. Go to **101**.

50

Yes, Mozart was at one time a batman and a singer; Amadeus a private eye and a vampire-trainer; and Wolf-fang a forger and a cardsharp.

Bludsucker looks at his watch. "Gad!" he explodes. "Must remember to reset my watch to Swahili time. Like they do in these parts of Africa. The Swahili day," he explains, "is literally the daylight hours which, on the Equator, run from sunrise, 7 a.m., to sunset, 7 p.m. They call 7 a.m. the first hour or 1 o'clock."

What time will it be by a Swahili clock when it is 5 p.m. European time?

If you think it is 11 o'clock,   go to **3**
If you think it is 10 o'clock,   go to **91**
Or if you think it is 12 o'clock, go to **57**.

N glances over your answers: "19, 25, 6. They add up to 50. Good word power. Any good at figures?"

"Try me, sir!"

"Let's see . . ." N leans back in his swivel chair and nearly tips over. "Oh yes . . . Let's say you have the same small change in your pocket as I have. How much should you give me so I've got 10 pence more than you?"

N idly types the problem into his slick, all-white desk-top computer. He peers at the green figures thrown up on the shiny screen.

If you think the answer is 10p, give it to him and go to **114**.

If you think the answer is 5p, go to **56**.

If you give up, go to **128**.

You'll have to earn your tip by working this out!

Which was a witch's *familiar*?

Her black hat?   Go to **135**
Her black cat?   Go to **141**
Her long broom?   Go to **48**.

No, that would be spelt solaR, with an R. Go back to **81**.

Before you can guess again, try your luck at this puzzle.

You fall asleep and have a nightmare. In it you see half a dozen Count Jugulas. Which is the odd one out?

1

2

3

4

5

6

Is it Number 1?   Go to **79**.
Is it Number 2?   Go to **94**.
Is it Number 3?   Go to **161**.
Is it Number 4?   Go to **143**.
Is it Number 5?   Go to **163**.
Is it Number 6?   Go to **95**.

Yes, it is number trickery. Here's how it goes. Writing a three-figure number twice is the same as multiplying it by 1001. Check: 286, 286 = 286 × 1001. BUT 1001 = 7 × 11 × 13. So when Bludsucker asked you to divide your 6-figure number by 7, 11, and 13 in turn he was really asking you to divide it by 1001. Which gives back your original number. On with the show! And go on to **108**.

You gain N's approval.

You give him 5p and he pockets it. You're now down 5p and he's up 5p. So he's got 10p more than you.

"That's what the computer says!" N smiles. "So it *must* be right. Ha-ha! You'll do. Let me put you in the picture, Alex. It is Alex, isn't it?"

You nod, adding, "And this is Mugs."

"Count Jugula's on the warpath again," N continues smoothly, swinging round idly in his swivel chair. "My spies report that he is hell-bent on World Domination again."

You give a squeaky whistle of surprise. Equally surprised, N looks down at his chair.

"Funny!" he frowns. "Shouldn't need oiling. It's brand new. Where were we? . . . Oh yes, Count Jugula is after the famous Egyptian Scarab that holds the secret of World Power. He will stop at nothing to possess it. We at the Spy Circus thought the Scarab was lost in the sands of the desert. You realize, don't you, that if Count Jugula gets his claws on the Scarab he will become more powerful than Hitler and Ghengis Khan put together? By the way, he is throwing everything he's got into the field –

Bludsucker, his bloodthirsty butler; Mara Harti, the beautiful international lady spy *and* his dastardly spies Mozart, Amadeus and Wolf-fang."

"But didn't we put the Mozart Trio away for good," you blurt out, "in Wormwood Scrubs?"

N is not best pleased by your keen question. "True, Alex, we did, we did. But Jugula's vampires sprang the Mozart Trio today. They are now in Rome. Get out there and get them! But don't let Jugula get the Scarab! Understood?" He flings you a latex face mask of Mozart himself. "May come in handy." You pocket the mask.

You and Mugs tiptoe out of his vast office to solve the weighty problem of retrieving the Scarab. You leave N to the weightier problem of weighing his finger in the goldfish bowl . . .

Back home, you and Mugs pack. You book a morning flight to Rome by phone.

"Better get a good night's sleep," you say to Mugs.

The time is 7 p.m. You set your radio alarm for 8.15 a.m. And you both fall into a deep sleep.

How much sleep do you get?

12 hours and a quarter? Go to **30**.

Longer? Go to **62**.

Shorter? Go to **138**.

57

No. Here's a tip: Think of the hour hand as having a tail and see where it points. When the hour hand points to 5, its tail points to . . . Go back to **50**.

You reach the minaret just in time to see Mozart leap into a taxi. Mugs races up to the old banger and overhears him direct the taxi-driver. "Take me to the . . ."

But Mugs does not catch the last word. All he can bark at you is something that sounds like "hoodwinks".

Where do you think Mozart is off to?

The Ice Rink?   Go to **100**

To have some iced drinks?   Go to **176**

To the nice Sphinx?   Go to **149**.

No, it is a period of time. Go to **55**.

Here's a clue: X = 6. Try again at **12**.

Yes, you would have *seen* the smoke before Mugs could hear the shot, and certainly before the bullet hit the water. Why? Because light travels faster than sound – or a bullet. You and Mugs go to your cabins and go to sleep. Move to **38**.

Tricky one, this. Don't lose any sleep over it – just go to **125**.

You mentally turn the inner triangle round through a third of a full turn. It now looks like this:

"Elementary, my dear Mugs!" you whoop with joy. "The big triangle is exactly four times as big as the small one. Four little ones fit neatly into the big one."

"But that means . . ." Mugs begins.

"Murder . . ." you whisper.

Just then there is a horrifying shriek from the deck cabins. You rush on deck to find Bludsucker, Amadeus and Wolf-fang milling around. You whip off your Mozart mask and pretend to be a detective.

"Mara's been stabbed to death," Bludsucker blurts out.

You ask each of them questions. Later, downstairs in the bar, you go through the facts you've discovered with

Mugs. You draw a plan of the cabins which you number 1 to 5, like this:

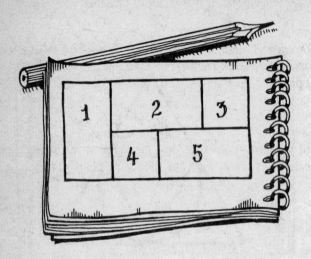

The facts are:

A Bludsucker's cabin is next to Wolf-fang's and has only two neighbouring cabins.

B Mara's cabin is next to Wolf-fang's and is bigger than Bludsucker's.

C The murderer's and Mara's cabins each have three adjoining cabins.

D Wolf-fang's and Amadeus's cabins are the same size.

E Wolf-fang's cabin has four neighbouring cabins.

If you think the murderer is
Bludsucker, go to **27**.
Amadeus, go to **142**.
Mozart, go to **111**.
Wolf-fang, go to **118**.

No, the answer is pyramid. Now go back to **23**.

Common enough mistake to make, Alex. It looks like you worked out (wrongly) that he made two lots of profits of 10 piastres at each deal. Go back to **31**.

Got your sums wrong, Alex. Go back to **19**. Clue: 598 means FLY. Now the sum should be plain sailing.

No, the answers were: bicycle, Liquid Crystal Display and Smackbot. Now return to **38**.

No. The answers were: Countess, Thirty-nine and gander. Go back to **56** and have another go.

"How many times did you try?" N asks.
    "Dozens of times," you reply.
    "One dozen will do. And that's a clue." N says.
    Go back to **138**.

Yes, Room 4. And this is the reasoning:

Fact A tells you that Bludsucker cannot be in cabins 2, 4 or 5 so he must be in cabins 1 or 3.

Fact B tells you that Mara must be in cabins 1, 2 or 5 (and therefore Bludsucker must be in cabin 3 since that is smaller).

Fact C tells you that Mara must be in cabin 5 since only cabins 4 and 5 have three adjoining rooms and cabin 4 is the same size as Bludsucker's.

Fact D tells you that Wolf-fang and Amadeus are in cabins 1 or 2 since Mara is in cabin 5.

Fact E tells you that Wolf-fang can only be in cabin 2 and therefore Amadeus is in cabin 1.

This leaves only room 4 unaccounted for and therefore that must have been Mozart's.

You hear voices in the distance..

"Well, good riddance, I say." Bludsucker says. "Never liked the woman. Far too vampish. And vampirish."

You quickly slip on the latex mask of Mozart. And Bludsucker strolls in.

"Well done, Mozart!" Bludsucker calls out to you. "I take it you did the doughty deed."

"How long does it take to get to Luxor?" you ask casually like a practised murderer who's "dunnit" again. "Well now," Bludsucker wheezes as he settles himself in a leather armchair. "The boat goes twice as fast downstream as it does up stream. It takes 10 hours less to make the trip up from Memphis to Luxor as it does downstream. I think that gives you the time it takes."

How long is the journey to Luxor?

Is it 10 hours, go to **13**

Is it 20 hours, go to **31**

Or is it 30 hours, go to **41**

71

Feel free to think it, Alex but, sssh!, don't say it. Well, not in front of N if you want to keep your job. Go back to **1**.

72

A phoney argument at work, Alex! Got your profits and losses muddled up. Go back to **31**.

73

Hope you didn't do too much number-scrunching. You've been had! Go back to **11**. To get the answer you must be TENacious!

74

No. Go to **23**.

75

Before you can guess again, answer this.
    Which of these is not a planet?
Mars Earth Venus Mercury Saturn Jupiter Plato

Mars?	Go to **157**
Earth?	Go to **166**
Venus?	Go to **168**
Mercury?	Go to **156**
Saturn?	Go to **158**
Jupiter?	Go to **165**
Plato?	Go to **153**

Yes, seven gloves.

Bludsucker goes to the looking glass. He borrows a lipstick from Mara Harti. On the glass he draws a couple of triangles – equal-sided things – one inside a circle, one outside, like this:

Mara screams. "Tell me, Bludsucker," she shrieks, "is the bigger triangle four times as big as the smaller one?"

Bludsucker looks puzzled. This interruption is clearly not part of his act. "I don't know . . ." he stammers.

"Because if it is," Mara howls, "it is a sign of MURDER!" With that she rushes from the bar.

"Time to pack it in," Amadeus says. "I'm toddling off to bed."

And the bar empties, leaving you and Mugs to stare at

Bludsucker's strange sign.

"I wonder . . ." you say quietly. "*Is* it four times as big?"

Can you tell without doing any "heavy" maths? Then go to **63**.

Is it too hard to work out?   Go to **18**.

77

No. The answers were: Countess, Thirty-nine and gander. Go back to **56** and have another go.

78

"C'mon, Mugs!" you yell. "Luxor, here we come!" You see a waiting taxi.

"Cairo! The railway station!" you tell the driver. "And fast!"

You leave the pyramids and the Sphinx in a cloud of dust and a taxi.

As the jalopy bumps along the left bank of the Nile back into town, you explain to Mugs what your plans are. "Before we can get to Luxor – that's where the Valley of the Kings is – we must pass through Memphis. We might catch Bludsucker between here and Memphis. Trouble is there are so many routes he can go by."

You produce a railway map of the region.

How many ways are there for Bludsucker to go by train from Cairo to Memphis. The trains all go left to right – no shunting backwards!

Go to the section with the same number as the number of ways.

Need help? Go to **42**.

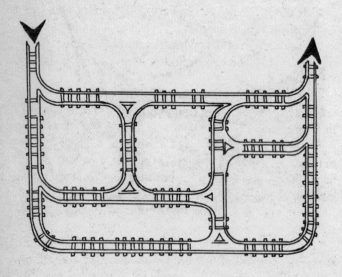

79

No, it was Number 6. Now move back to **3**.

80

Go to **9**.

You mimic Mozart perfectly. What an artist you are! He notices nothing out of the ordinary. He turns to greet Mara Harti.

"Recovered from your camel ride?" she replies.

"Camel ride?" Mozart asks. He looks nonplussed. "Never been on one."

"But I rode with you just now," she says. "At Memphis."

"Memphis?" Mozart splutters. "Tennessee?"

"MOZART," she bawls, "are you drunk?"

"No," he replies blankly.

"Then you aren't the Mozart I know," she hisses.

"Gad!" Bludsucker explodes like a Colonel Blimp. "An imposter!"

"Stand up the *real* Mozart!" Amadeus yells.

The real Mozart can't take any more. He bolts from the bar room.

Bludsucker's bleery eyes fall on you. "Ah, here's my real friend. Good ol' Mozy!" And he claps you on the back like a long-lost chum. He whispers to you, "Don't give me away, old boy. I'm travellin' incognito."

"I thought," you reply, "we were travelling in a paddle steamer."

"I say, I say," Bludsucker bellows like a fair-ground barker, waving his pith helmet in the air. "Anyone tell me why me hat's called a *sola* topee? *Topee* means *hat*, like topper. But what does *sola* mean?"

If you think it's to do with the sun, go to **53**

If you think it means *lonely* or *solo*, go to **124**

If you think it is the Indian word for pith, go to **46**.

Fooled you! No, go to **54**.

No, your sums are wrong, Alex. Work out what the differences are between next-door numbers on the dial. Before you try again, go to **35**.

Wrong room. Go back to **111**.

No, your thinking is fishy! Go back to **1**.

No, wrong key. Go to **75**.

Wrong. Think about this carefully but before you can try again, go to **101**.

No, funnier than that. It's a pun. Go back to **90**.

Yes, a silkworm is a moth. Now have another try at **58**.

This is how Bludsucker made three squares from nine matches:

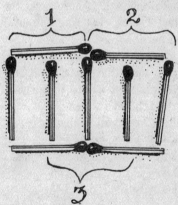

"Neat, isn't it?" Bludsucker says. "By the way, heard the story of the lion who got into the Houses of Parliament and ate the Prime Minister. Can you guess what time it was?"

Midday?   Go to **88**
20 hours?   Go to **102**
Lunchtime?   Go to **126**.

No. Here's a tip: Think of the hour hand as having a tail and see where it points. When the hour hand points to 5, its tail points to . . . Go back to **50**.

Well done! You and Mugs leave the maze by Exit A. Here a short flight of steps leads you down to a burial chamber. In the middle of its stone floor you see by torch light a glittering, gold box. Engraved on its shining flat top are the words:

THE SECRET OF WORLD POWER

You give a low whistle. "*This* must be what Count Jugula is after! Quick, we must open it before his henchmen get here, Mugs!"

You try to prise the box open to get at the prize shut inside. It is firmly locked. Mugs whines and sniffs up at a bunch of keys hanging on a hook in the wall. You take the bunch. You try each key in turn.

Which of these keys will fit the lock?

If you think key A fits, go to **140**
If you think key B fits, go to **86**
If you think key C fits, go to **105**
If you think key D fits, go to **145**

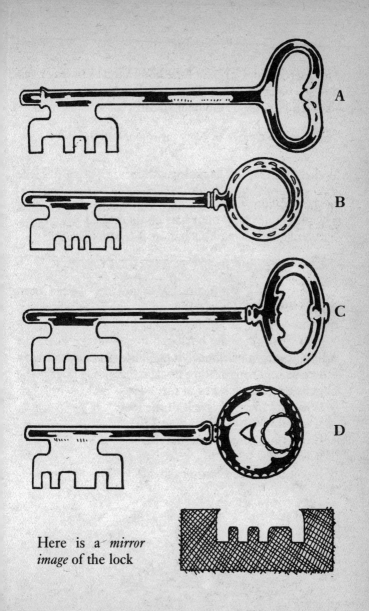

A

B

C

D

Here is a *mirror image* of the lock

93

No. 4 won't give a whole number of cats. Go back to **46**.

94

No, it was Number 6. Now move back to **3**.

95

Correct. All the Counts that are smiling have raised hats. The glum ones have their hats on their head. Number 6 has a smiling face and his hat on. Now go back to **3**.

96

Try again at **120**.

97

No, those were the jobs of Amadeus. Go back to **116**.

"Yes," you say proudly.

"Yes what?" N says testily. "Yes, SIR!" you say. "Your finger takes up space. This raises the water level. So if the bowl were on scales the scales would read higher."

"Really?" N says. "Good thinking." And he flings a typewritten sheet at you. "Complete that! Just a little test we like to give spy-catchers. To test your word power."

The test paper looks like this:

What do these words mean? Note the numbers of your answers and add them up.

REPARTEE:
a party-goer (27)   a witty retort (19)   a golfing term (9)

INTRICATE:
awkward (15)   implicate (21)   difficult to follow (25)

COMPLEMENT:
that which completes something (6)   flattery (3)   given away free (30)   charming agreement (12)

If you score 50,   go to **51**
If 40–49,   go to **119**
If over 50,   go to **107**.

No, your sums are wrong, Alex. You need to work out the differences between next-door numbers on the dial. But before you can try again, go to **35**.

It should have been the Sphinx. But before you set off you must complete this puzzle.

What is a silkworm?

a worm?   Go to **150**
a butterfly? Go to **24**
a moth?   Go to **89**.

You must answer this puzzle before you can try again. Moses sent ten plagues upon the people of Egypt at the time of the Pharaohs. Which of these was *not* a plague?

Frogs?   Go to **160**
Locusts? Go to **106**
Snakes? Go to **151**
Flies?   Go to **164**.

Yes, 20 hours or 8 p.m. Ate P.M., geddit?

"Well, I'm off to bed," Bludsucker yawns and goes on deck to his cabin. Amadeus and Wolf-fang follow suit, leaving you and Mugs in the bar. You both wander on deck to enjoy the cool night air and to stargaze. The Arab Scarab-seller comes on deck. Suddenly there is a shot from the bank of the Nile. The shot strikes the water quite near the paddle steamer. Mugs hears the shot. You see the puff of smoke. The Arab sees the bullet hit the water.

Which of you three knew that a gun had been fired?
Mugs first?   Go to **14**
You first?   Go to **61**
The Arab first? Go to **134**.

103

Here's a clue: S = 1. Try again at **12**.

104

No, Mozart would see through that! The wrong hand holds the comb. Go back to **15**.

105

No, wrong key. Go to **75**.

106

Snakes was the right answer. Now have another go at **147**.

107

You haven't got all of them right. Go back to **98**.

108

Bludsucker holds up his hand to still the deafening applause at his amazing number trick.

"Tell me," he says. "You have a drawerful of gloves – left-handed and right-handed, of course – and in three different colours: two pairs of Day-glo green, two pairs of sickly orange gloves and two pairs of blinding yellow gloves. You go to get out the gloves and, as before, the lights fuse. So you have to get out the gloves in the dark. How few do you need to make sure of getting a pair the same colour, one left-hand glove, one right-hand glove, of course."

If you think the answer is 5 gloves, go to **22**
If you think it is 6 gloves, go to **36**
Or if you think it is 7 gloves, go to **76**.

109

Good shooting. 38 it is. First you add 6 to 2, then 8, then 10, then 12 and then 14.

You take aim and fire. You see the *S.S. Titania* go up in

a great plume of flame and smoke.

"That's the last we shall see of Count Jugula and his gang," you say.

Later in London, N congratulates you and Mugs on another good job done. The pair of you pat yourselves on the back – well, you pat Mugs on his back – and take a well-earned rest.

Yes, they are all African animals. You follow the tracks of the army lorry in your Cessna. You land and spot a sheet of paper.

"Hullo," you say. "Another clue."

You read the sheet of paper which has fallen out of the count's departing lorry. It says:

Find the other half of these well-known phrases. Put the answers in the numbered rows of boxes and the arrowed column will read where you must go next.

1. rant and ——
2. eat and ——
3. chop and ——
4. give and ——
5. come and ——
6. hope and ——
7. stand and —— (highwayman's words)
8. tooth and ——

Where do you go next?

cataract?   Go to **171**
Victoria?   Go to **113**
pyramids?   Go to **123**.

111

Give yourself a pat on the back. Yes, Mozart did the foul deed. After all, he had a motive as Mara was foul about him.

Which room was the murder committed in?

Room 1, go to **8**
Room 2, go to **47**
Room 3, go to **84**
Room 4, go to **70**
Room 5, go to **154**.

112

Turn again, Dick Whittington! Go to **131**.

"Victoria—" you exclaim. "That must mean Lake Victoria!"

Now go to **39**.

N pockets your ten pence coin and says, "Wrong!" Go back to **51**.

You have heard enough.

"We must blow Count Jugula out of the water!" you say to Mugs. You set up the portable EXOCET missile N has provided you with. You check the direction and range. This means, in effect, working out the next number on the dial shown here. It has been scratched off the dial by mistake. What should it be?

If you think the range number is 40,   go to **83**
If you think it is 38,   go to **109**
Or if you think it is 36,   go to **99**.

10 piastres it is.

Just then a violent argument breaks out between Bludsucker and the barman. They are arguing about what jobs Mozart, Amadeus and Wolf-fang have done in the course of their spying duties for Count Jugula. You lie low in order not to attract Bludsucker's attention – in your Mozart mask.

The jobs they've taken between them are: private eye, vampire-trainer, singer, *bat*man(!), forger, and card-sharp. Can you work out each spy's two jobs from these facts you overhear?

A The forger took the vampire-trainer's vampish girl-friend to a Halloween party.

B Both the vampire-trainer and the singer like bloodsucking with Wolf-fang.

C The batman often drank with the forger.

D Amadeus owes the singer a tenner. Naturally, the singer is a tenor!

E The vampire-trainer was a private eye.

What you think were Mozart's jobs:

  a batman and a singer?   Go to **50**
  a private eye and a vampire-trainer?   Go to **97**
  a forger and a cardsharp?   Go to **133**.

117

You've lost your way. Go back to **149** and try again.

118

No he didn't. Go back to **63**.

119

You can't have got them all right, Alex. Back you go to 98.

120

"160 metres," you say. "Hmm, looks higher from here. It's shorter than the Hilton."

"'C'mon!" Mugs barks. Just then there is a thud at the hotel room door. You open it. Stuck in the woodwork is a note. It is pinned by a . . .

dagger!

You pull the note free and hurriedly scan it.

"Drat!" you curse. "And double drat! It's in code."

This is what it says:

Find the missing word in each phrase. Write it in its numbered box below. Do the puzzle and the arrowed column spells where you go next.

1 —— in the bud (cut off)

2 On the —— (definitely not)

3 Face the —— (meet the worst)

4 Smell a — (be suspicious)

5 —— one's trumpet (boast)

6 Take —— winks (kip)

7 —— of one, half a dozen of the other (no difference)

Where do you have to go: the post box? Go to **162**
the pyramid? Go to **96**
the minaret? Go to **152**.

You whizz off to the first cataract on the Nile. No Count Jugula! You hire a small Cessna monoplane and fly around looking for the Count's speeding lorry with its crew of Bludsucker and the Mozart Trio AND the precious Scarab beetle.

You are about to land for a night's stop when you radio base to know which animals are likely to be roaming about. The chap at the other end sends you the list *in code*! For secrecy's sake.

This is his message. Can you find an animal hidden in each sentence?

1 You say you twice rang the bell? I only heard it once.
2 Flags fluttered in the breeze, brass bands played and the sun shone brightly.
3 Caramel and toffee
   Are sweeter than coffee
4 Get the post, Richard!
5 A cold at the weekend is as bad as catarrh in office time.

Were the animals all African wild beasts?   Go to **110**
Were they all domestic pets?   Go to **17**
Or were they all birds?   Go to **34**.

No, you were fooled by all the Pi R squared gobbledegook! Go to **25**.

No. Try again at **110**.

Well . . . you *can* call a single, lone woman singer *sola*. Go back to **81**.

Before you can have another attempt at **56**, see if you can do any better with this puzzle.
What is the female of Earl?
Duchess (17)   Marchioness (19)   Countess (15)

How many steps in John Buchan's famous thriller?
Twenty-nine (21)   Thirty-nine (23)   Fifty-nine (17)

Sauce for the goose is sauce for the . . .?
Panda (15)   Gander (17)   Gosling (19)

Add up your answers.
If you scored 50 go to **68**
If you scored 53 go to **77**
If you scored 55 go to **43**

No, funnier than that. It's a pun. Go back to **90**.

Here are the 18 names:
Ann, Lulu, Anna, Diana, Dianne, Dinah, Edna, Hannah, Lena, Jennie, Mary, Minnie, Mae, Mia, Nan, Nancy, Jane and Judy. Now go back to **108**.

128

"Give up?" N barks curtly. "Give me your small change. Now go back to **51** and try again."

129

Good thinking!

"No chance at all," Bludsucker says.

"Why ever not?" Amadeus pipes up.

"Because," Bludsucker says, "if two of the men have their own hat on, then so must the third. So it's impossible for *only* two to have their own hat on. All three must have."

There is a general gasp of astonishment.

"For my next trick," Bludsucker announces, "I want you all – Mozart, that includes you. Get a paper and pencil NOW! – to jot down any three-figure number. Then repeat the three figures in the same order. You should now have a six-figure number. Like, say, 286, 286. But you choose your own." (That goes for you Alex, gentle reader!) "Now divide your number by 7. Use a calculator or your cuff, ha-ha! No need to worry about a remainder: there won't be one."

"What a mind-reader!" Amadeus gasps.

"Done that?" Bludsucker asks. "For example, my 286, 286 divided by 7 is 40898 exactly. No remainder. See? Now divide your result by 11. Again I predict there will be no remainder."

"He's right, dash it!" Wolf-fang gasps.

(For example, 40898 divided by 11 is 3718.)

"Finally," Bludsucker announces, "I want you all to divide your last result by 13. Again, no remainder."

(For example, 3718 divided by 13 is 286.)

Amadeus nearly falls off his bar stool with surprise. "He's not wrong, you know," he exclaims.

"Amazed?" Bludsucker asks. "Well, you ain't seen nuttin' yet! Your final result is none other than . . .
Well, what is it?

Your original three-figure number? Go to **16**.
Twice your original number? Go to **7**.
Half your original number? Go to **44**.

130

Well done! Have another try now at **38**.

131

You find another note. Must have fallen out of Mozart's pocket. It's a riddle-me-ree telling you where to go.

My first is in POTATO but not in TOMATO.

My second is in THYME but not in TIME.

My third is in FIRE but not in FLAME.
My fourth is in AYE but not in OYEZ.
My fifth is in ROME but not in NERO.
My sixth is in KING but not in KONG.
My seventh is in SAND but not in CASTLE.
Am I an ancient Egyptian stone structure? Go to **172**.
Am I an ancient Egyptian fire-eater? Go to **64**.

132

Yes, you are correct. Wanna know how Bludsucker's trick works? Go on to **55**.

133

No, those were the jobs of Wolf-fang. Go back to **116**.

No, try again. Back to **102**.

No, it is black cat. Now go back to **9** and have another look at that code.

Need a tip? (A felt tip maybe?) This isn't it. Go to **52**.

No. A light year is a distance. Now go on to **55**.

Yes, you sleep for only an hour and a quarter. The alarm clock wakes you at 8.15 p.m. *the same evening*!

You fly to Rome with Mugs. You land at Leonardo da Vinci airport. After passing through customs you spot a man in dark glasses and a slouch hat. He is reading a slip of paper. It is Mozart!

On your orders, Mugs bounds up to him and paws him like a long-lost master. Mozart tries to push Mugs away. Mugs snaps up the paper and brings it to you. The pair of you slip away into the crowd.

In a quiet side-street café you read the slip of paper. It is cut from Count Jugula. It says:

"Go to Left Luggage Locker Number . . . at Leonardo airport. To find the number answer the following questions and put your answers in the boxes. The key letters in the bold squares will spell out the number of the locker where you will find a message waiting for you."

"We must solve this quickly," you say to Mugs, producing a pencil.

The paper reads:

1 What's the opposite of "not out"?

2 Can you make a useful piece of office equipment from these letters: RTEYEWPIRT?

3 While checking the stock of a toy shop the bookkeeper noticed that the word "balloon" had two sets of double letters, one after the other.

"I wonder," he said to himself, "if there is an English word with *three* sets of double letters, one right after the other?"

Write it here:

Clue: The word is on this sheet.

4 Cross out six letters here:

RASPBPRLNEY

so that the remaining letters, in the same order, spell a

fruit. Write it here:

Slide the four strips up or down until a four-letter word shows in the frame:

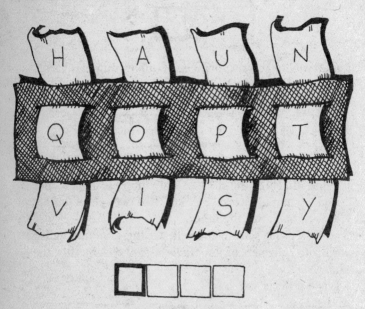

Rearrange the letters of NEW DOOR to make two new words.

Put the letters in the thick boxes in order here. What do they spell? The locker number is . . .

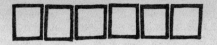

Go to that section.

Or would you like N to tell you where to go? (Politely, of course!) Then go to **69**.

139

No so, Alex. Wolf-fang has only got to count out the coins and see how many *more* 2-piastre coins there are than 1-piastre coins. That number is the number of the arcade machines to the right where the dead letter drop is. Go back to **162** and try again.

140

You put key A in the lock. You turn it. Yes, it fits! But before you have had time to open the golden box, you feel an icy claw grip your shoulder.

You wheel round.

"Bludsucker!" you gasp. And you find yourself staring into the steady eye of a gun.

"Put that down!" he rasps. "Oh, and put them up!"

You put up two shaking hands in the stuffy air. You glance over your shoulder into the gloom. Mugs is lying doggo.

The gun jabs you in the ribs.

"Up those steps—" the gun's owner hisses.

You take a few steps towards the steps.

"Not so fast!" Bludsucker grates out. "First, a little puzzle. You note, do you not, that there are eight steps, not counting the landing at the top. Starting from the stone floor, you must land twice on the landing, stopping there at the finish, after you have returned once to this floor. But you must use each step the same number of times.

What are the fewest moves you can take to get up to the landing (one step includes stepping up or down)? You'd better number the steps in order, upward, 1 to 8."

What's the fewest moves you can do it in?

19 moves? Go to **19**
21 moves? Go to **26**
25 moves? Go to **144**.

141

Yes, you're correct. Now go back to **9** and have another look at that Sphinx pattern.

142

No he didn't. Go back to **63**.

No, it was Number 6. Now move on to 3.

No, fewer moves. Step lively! This is the rule: you return to the floor after the first step; then go three steps up for one step down. Go back to **140**.

No, wrong key. Go to **75**.

Yes, there's the sphinx buried cunningly in A: fly on.

You and Mugs land at Cairo. As you step out on the tarmac the heat hits you. A taxi ride brings you to the towering Hilton Hotel. A bell-boy shows you up to the top floor where a room overlooking west Cairo awaits you. You gaze across at Giza and the Great Pyramids there.

"Gosh, they must be tall!" you say.

"Wanna know how tall the Great Pyramid is? I tell you!" says the bell-boy. "If the Great Pyramid was five times taller it would be as high as the Hilton is – if the Hilton were four times as high as it is. Which it isn't! The Hilton is **200** metres."

He shouts the last words and holds out his hand again. You give him a 200–piastre tip and he gives you a smile . . . leaving you to puzzle out the height of the Great Pyramid.

If you think it is 160 metres, go to **120**

If you think it is 150 metres, go to **159**.

147

"Two cats it is!" Bludsucker cries, peeping into the hat. He is now well in his stride as a Magicman. "For my next trick," he goes on without *pause*, saying *purr*posively, "I'd like you *all*, each and everyone of you, to watch my sola topee *very closely* – and that includes *you*, Mozart!" (He, of course, means you, Alex.) Then he goes on.

"Abracadabra! Sim-sala- BRIM!" He turns the inside of his hat towards his audience for you all to see.

It is empty!

A *cat*aract of applause greets this *cat*aclysmic

disappearing act. The question on everyone's lips is: "How did he make the cats vanish into thin air?"

"Now comes the tricky part," Bludsucker says, bowing. "Talking of hats, say three people go to a party. The lights fuse. They grab their hats in the dark. What is the chance that exactly two of them – *and only two* will be wearing his own hat?"

If you think it is a dead cert, go to **49**

If you think there is no chance at all, go to **129**

Or if you think there is a one-in-three chance, go to **87**.

148

No, it's not mind-reading. But Bludsucker and the author are very flattered if you think it *is*! Go to **55** and see how it's done.

149

"Obviously," you yell over the traffic's din. "The Sphinx!" You and Mugs grab a cab and set off for Giza, where the Sphinx and the Great Pyramid are.

Dusty and shaken and hot you arrive at Giza. You pay the taxi off. But no Mozart! He may be in the milling crowds. Round them are swarms of guides, buzzing like flies round fruit ripe for plucking. One of them oils his way up to you.

"You like see inside Greatest Pyramid?" he whines.

You brush him off like a fly. Mugs sends him on his way with a friendly snarl. Quickly you make your way across the sand to the enormous stone statue of the Sphinx. You work your way round to the south paw of the Sphinx. One of the claws has a sliding panel in it. You find a waxy knob. You press it. The panel slides open.

Inside is a dark chamber.

Quickly you and Mugs slip inside. You switch on your High-Beam torch. You slide the panel to. The torch beam lights up a maze of passages.

Here is a picture of them. Can you thread your way through?

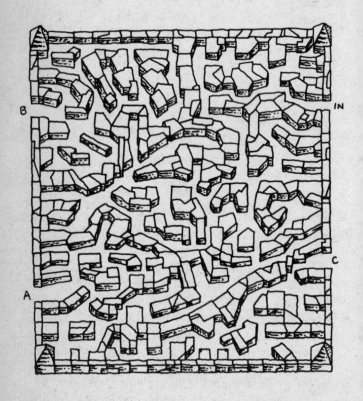

Do you come out at Exit A?   Then go to **92**
       Exit B?   Go to **21**
       Exit C?   Go to **117**.

150

No, it is a moth. Try again at **58**.

151

Correct. Now have another go at **147**.

152

Try again at **120**.

153

Yes. Plato was a philosopher. The others are all planets. Now go to **92** and try again.

154

Wrong room. Go back to **111**.

155

No, the answers were: bicycle, Liquid Crystal Display and Smackbot. Now return to **38**.

156

Wrong. Plato was a philosopher. The others are all planets. Now go to **92** and continue your quest.

157

Wrong. Plato was a philosopher. The others are all planets. Now go to **92** and continue your quest.

158

Wrong. Plato was a philosopher. The others are all planets. Now go to **92** and continue your quest.

159

No. Go back to **146**.

160

Snakes was the right answer. Now have another go at **147**.

161

No, it was Number 6. Now go back to **3**.

162

You nip down to the ground floor of the Hilton. In the foyer you spot the Post Box. It is bang outside the Hotel Tea Room. You pop your head in and who should you see but Mozart and Amadeus. But no Wolf-fang!

You slide into an empty chair at a table behind an aspidistra. You keep watch on the spies through the long green fronds.

"You sure Wolf-fang knows?" Mozart hisses.

"Knows?" Amadeus asks blankly.

"Where the dead letter drop is, dolt!"

"Behind the Space Invaders Machine," Amadeus says, "in the Amusement Arcade."

"Ssssh!" Mozart bellows. "Someone may be listening in."

The whole tea room stops talking to listen in.

"How are we going to let Wolf-fang know which one, Mozart?"

"I've thought of that, Amadeus. We'll leave him a message in coin code."

Mozart draws a plan of the Amusement Arcade:

"I've numbered the machines with code numbers," Mozart says. "Prime numbers, actually."

He produces a pile of coins from his overcoat pocket and drops them on the table. He sorts the coins into two neat piles. "One–piastre coins. And two–piastre coins. Right? Now each one–piastre coin stands for a move of one arcade machine to the left. And a two–piastre coin stands for a move of one arcade machine to the right. Wolf-fang knows we always count from the Cash Desk. Right?"

Amadeus nods.

"To confuse any double-agents I'll leave a tip. In several piles of coins."

"Like in all the best spy stories, eh?" Amadeus asks.

"Listen!" Mozart snaps. "Wolf-fang will then look at this pile of 1–piastre coins.

Mozart counts out four 1–piastre coins on the gingham table cloth.

"Which tells him to move four Space Invader Machines to the left."

Mozart pays out three 2–piastre coins next to the pile

of 1–piastre coins. He says:

"Wolf-fang then marches three machines to the right again."

"Because the three 2–piastre coins tell him to," Amadeus says. "I get it!"

"THEN . . ." Mozart places a pile of two 1–piastre coins next to the piles already on the tablecloth. "These two coins tell him to go back to the left by two machines."

Mozart puts down another pile of five 2–piastre coins. "Finally, he counts another five machines to the right, including the Cash Desk from where he last landed up, of course."

"That should put any spy-catchers off the scent," Amadeus says gleefully.

Mozart leaves the neat piles of coins as a tip under a plate. At that moment Wolf-fang swings through the doors of the tea rooms. Mozart and Amadeus get up quickly and pass Wolf-fang on their way out. They wink heavily at him.

You lean across to their table and mix up the coins.

"Heh, heh!" you laugh to Mugs. "That'll fool Wolf-fang."

But *will* it? You have second thoughts. Which Space Invaders Machine will Wolf-fang go to?

Go to the section of that number.

If you think it'll fool Wolf-fang, go to **139**.

163

No, it was Number 6. Now go back to **3**.

164

Snakes was the right answer. Now go back to **147**.

Wrong. Plato was a philosopher. The others are all
planets. Now go to **92** and continue your quest.

166

Wrong. Plato was a philosopher. The others are all planets. Now go to **92** and continue your quest.

167

No, there are more than that. Here are the 18 names: Ann, Lulu, Anna, Diana, Dianne, Dinah, Edna, Hannah, Lena, Jennie, Mary, Minnie, Mae, Mia, Nan, Nancy, Jane, and Judy.

Now go back to **108**.

168

Wrong. Plato was a philosopher. The others are all planets. Now go to **92** and continue your quest.

169

You say, "What did you say?" and the native merely repeats what he said. And you are none the wiser. Go back to **35**.

170

Yes, the sum is:

$$
\begin{array}{r}
62410 \\
+\ 53981 \\
\hline
116391
\end{array}
$$

On the back of the slip of paper you read this message in code:
100 986 2850 45 1234561 289

What do the numbers stand for? Go back to **12** and work it out. Then you can decode these numbers, can't

you? 5450
   Go to the section with this number. Need help? Go to **80**.

171

No. Try again at **110**.

172

Yes, a pyramid. Now try again at **23**.

173

Yes, because if the lily doubles its size every hour and covers the lake in 25 hours, it will only cover half the lake an hour earlier. Go to **115**.

174

No. Before you try again, see if you can do better with this one:
   Note the numbers of your answers and add them up.

Which Queen of England reigned the longest?
Queen Elizabeth I (4)   Elizabeth II (16)   Victoria (26)   Mary (28)
Who discovered the West Indies?
Vasco da Gama (13)   Magellan (22)   Christopher Columbus (20)
Who painted the 'Mona Lisa'?
Leonardo da Vinci (7)   Michaelangelo (31)   Raphael (10)

If you score 57, go to **178**
If you score 53, go to **130**.

Wrong place, I think. Go back to **45**.

176

Wrong place. Go to **100** to find the correct answer.

177

A catapult isn't a place. You can't be thinking, Alex. Go back to **45**.

178

No. The correct answers are Victoria, Christopher Columbus and Leonardo da Vinci. Go to **38**.

CHEATS' GUIDE ONLY

Here are the correct answers to each of the puzzles.

1 The goldfish bowl will weigh more.

3 This diagram will show you how to make 3 squares from 9 matches.

7 It is number trickery. Writing a three-figure number twice is the same as multiplying it by 1001. When Bludsucker asks you to divide your six-figure number by 7, 11 and 13 he is really asking you to divide it by 1001 giving you your original number.

9 Pattern A contains the sphinx.

10 There are 15 differences.

11 There are 10 rungs showing above the water.

12
$$\begin{array}{r} 62410 \\ 53981 \ + \\ \hline 116391 \\ \hline \end{array}$$

Therefore HWS = 391.

15 Face B is the right reflection.

16 It is number trickery. Writing a three-figure number twice is the same as multiplying it by 1001. When Bludsucker asks you to divide your six-figure number by 7, 11 and 13 he is really asking you to divide it by 1001 giving you your original number.

19 The message tells you to 'GO TO LUXOR'.

23 The correct answers are: camel, notice, nick, fat, wrong, tea and tongue. In the diagram this spells MINARET.

25 There are 35 triangles in the witch's pentacle.

31 Bludsucker made 10 piastres profit.

33 The correct answers are bicycle, Liquid Crystal Display and smackbot which add up to 47.

35 You say, "Did you say 'Umbo'?" Whatever the native now replies will tell you which word means 'Yes'.

37 There are at least 18 names.

38 The soothsayer predicts the dagger. How does she do it? The trick depends on a single number fact: add the digits in your final answer and they will total a number that you can divide by 9. In fact the total will be 18. The reason for this we won't discuss as it would only *non-plus*!

39 The lily will cover half the lake in 24 hours. In a further hour it will have doubled in size and will cover the entire lake.

44 A light year is a measure of distance.

45 The correct answers are ocean, lead, master, laud, tutor, tear, copse and pest. In the diagram this spells CATARACT.

46 Bludsucker has 2 pretend "cats" in his hat.

50 When it's 5 p.m. European time it will be 11 o'clock by Swahili clock.

51 If you give N 5 pence he'll have 10 pence more than you.

52 A witch's familiar is her cat.

54 Number 6 is the odd one out.

56 You will have less than 12 and a quarter hours – in fact, you will get just one and a quarter hours since the alarm goes off at 8.15 p.m. that evening.

58 Mozart cries, "To the nice Sphinx!"

63 Mozart did the foul deed.

70 It takes 20 hours to travel to Luxor.

75 Plato is not a planet. He was a philosopher.

76 The big triangle is exactly four times as big as the smaller one. Mentally turn the inner triangle around one third of a full term to see how.

78 There are 11 ways for Bludsucker to reach Memphis by train.

81 *Sola* is the Indian word for *pith*.

90 It was 20 hours, or 8 p.m. [ATE (the) P.M. (Prime Minister!)]

92 Key A fits the lock.

98 The correct answers are repartee, intricate and complement which add up to 50.

100 A silkworm is a moth.

101 There was no plague of snakes.

102 *You* would have seen the smoke before Mugs heard the shot and the bullet hit the water.

108 You need to pull out 7 gloves to be sure of getting a pair the same colour.

110 The correct answers are rave, drink, change, take, go, pray, deliver and nail. In the diagram this spells VICTORIA.

111 The murder was committed in Room 4.

115 The correct number on the dial is 38.

116 Mozart was formerly a batman and a singer.

120 The correct answers are nip, contrary, music, rat, blow, forty and six. In the diagram this spells post box.

121 You will find lion, zebra, eland, ostrich and rhino if you look carefully. All these animals are African wild beasts.

125 The correct answers are countess, Thirty-nine and gander which adds up to 50.

129 It should be your original three-figure number.

131 The correct answer is pyramid.

138 The correct answers are out, typewriter, book-keeper, apple, vast and one word. In the diagram this spells TWELVE.

140 The manoeuvre can be done in 19 moves.

146 The Great Pyramid is 160 metres high.

147 There is no chance at all that only 2 of them will be wearing their own hat. If two of the men have the correct hats so must the third.

149 You emerge at Exit A.

162 Wolf-fang will go to the machine numbered 23.

174 The correct answers are Victoria, Christopher Columbus and Leonardo da Vinci whose numbers add up to 53.